William Henry Venable

Melodies of the Heart, Songs of Freedom

And Other Poems

William Henry Venable

Melodies of the Heart, Songs of Freedom
And Other Poems

ISBN/EAN: 9783744710374

Printed in Europe, USA, Canada, Australia, Japan

Cover: Foto ©Thomas Meinert / pixelio.de

More available books at **www.hansebooks.com**

MELODIES OF THE HEART

SONGS OF FREEDOM

AND OTHER POEMS

BY

W. H. VENABLE

*Author of "June on the Miami," "The Teacher's Dream,"
etc., etc.*

CINCINNATI
ROBERT CLARKE & CO
1885

TO MY WIFE.

*Wise, noble, **loved** and loving Wife,*
*These heart-born **songs**, a gift, I bring*
To thee, whose deeds, thy muses, sing
The poem of a perfect life.

CONTENTS.

MELODIES OF THE HEART.

	PAGE
SUMMER LOVE	13
ASHES	16
THE WEDDING DEFERRED	18
THE INEVITABLE	20
HINCHMAN'S MILL	22
THE TUNES DAN HARRISON USED TO PLAY	25
CHILD LOST	28

SONGS OF FREEDOM AND FAITH.

WE THE PEOPLE	35
THE VOICE OF ALL	40
THE VENAL VOTE	42
THE HOME FLAG	43
A TRIUNE CREED	45
NO CASTE IN BLOOD	48
THE SEEKING SOUL	50
BY THEIR FRUITS	51
REVELATION	52

CONTENTS.

AN OCTAVE OF SONNETS.

An India Shawl..........................
Plato..................................
Dante..................................
Carlyle................................
Wagner.................................
The Kaiser March.......................
Longfellow.............................
Unsung.................................

OCCASIONAL POEMS.

A Gentle Man...........................
Victor.................................
The Concord Seer.......................
The Poet of Clovernook.................
The Patriot's Meed.....................
A Gift Acknowledged....................
Forest Song............................

FOR MY CHILDREN.

The School Girl........................
Flora's Favorite.......................
The Sacred Snow........................
Fairy Land.............................
A Boy's Heaven.........................
The Readers............................
Wag....................................
Donatello..............................

CONTENTS.

ETCHINGS BY THE WAY.

	PAGE
THE OPEN SECRET	109
A SNOW BIRD	111
A WHARF RAT	113
THE UPSET	115
A MIRACLE	117
PROTOPLASM	118

IN THE LIBRARY.

WITH BOOKS	123
THE GENIUS OF THE PRESS	129
DEFOE IN THE PILLORY	131

MELODIES OF THE HEART.

SUMMER LOVE.

I KNOW 'tis late, but let me stay,
For night is tenderer than day;
Sweet love, dear love, I can not go;
Dear love, sweet love, I love thee so.
The birds are in the grove asleep,
The katydids shrill concert keep,
The woodbine breathes a fragrance rare,
To please the dewy, languid air,
The fire-flies twinkle in the vale,
The river shines in moonlight pale:
See yon bright star! choose it for thine,
And call its near companion mine;
Yon air-spun lace above the moon,—
'Twill vail her radiant beauty soon;
And look! a meteor's dreamy light
Streams mystic through the solemn night.

SUMMER LOVE.

Ah, life glides swift, like that still fire,
How soon our gleams of joy expire.
Who can be sure the present kiss
Is not his last? Make all of this.
I know 'tis late, dear love, I know,
Dear love, sweet love, I love thee so.

It can not be the stealthy day
That turns the orient darkness gray;
Heardst thou? I thought or feared I heard
Vague twitters of some wakeful bird.
Nay, 'twas but summer in her sleep
Low murmuring from the leafy deep.
Fantastic mist obscurely fills
The hollows of Kentucky hills.
The wings of night are swift indeed!
Why makes the jealous morn such speed?
This rose thou wear'st may I not take
For passionate remembrance' sake?
Press with thy lips its crimson heart.
Yes, blushing rose, we must depart.
A rose can not return a kiss—
I pay its due with this, and this.
The stars grow faint, they soon will die,
But love fades not nor fails. Good-bye!

SUMMER LOVE.

Unhappy joy—delicious pain—
We part in love, we meet again.
Good-bye!—the morning dawns—I go;
Dear love, sweet love, I love thee so.

ASHES.

THE fire of love is dead.
  No spark of living red
 The cold, gray ashes show.
Be still! thy sighing breath—
Can it requicken death?
  Nay, hope not, dream not so.
   Ah, no, no, no.

We thought love's fire eterne.
Alas! no more 't will burn.
  Nor glowing kiss, nor vow,
May kindle it again;
In vain! Tears, too, are vain.
  We love not, I nor thou.
   Ah, no, no, no.

ASHES.

Love's embers are gone out.
There is no hope for doubt.
    We once did love. Good-bye.
Cold ashes. Cold and gray.
Good-bye. We go love's way;
    Naught's left us but to die.
        Ah, no, no, no.

THE WEDDING DEFERRED.

COMPLAINING flow the waters slow
  Along the valley green and low;
The lilies dight in virgin white
Float fragrant in the ardent light,
And to the gossip ripples say,
"It is the Day;—is't not the Day?
When comes the bridal train this way?"

Yon amethystine hill-top kist
By lingering, enamored mist,
Hears in the sky warm zephyrs sigh
To wooing clouds that dally by;
The wandering whispers seem to say
"Is't not the Day?—it is the Day!
Why comes no bridal train this way?"

THE WEDDING DEFERRED.

Forlorn of mood, by love pursued,
A youth laments in solitude;
The brown dove's eyes soft sympathize
With him, and to her mate she cries,
"What can the glad espousals stay?
It is the Day;—is't not the Day?
No bridal train comes down this way.

No bridal train,—unhappy swain,
Thy lady's promises are vain."
Oh! birds, forbear, ye mated pair,
My absent, blameless darling spare;
Among her maids she mourns to say
"Is't not the Day?—it is the Day!
No bridal train comes down this way."

Oh! laggard moon, arise full soon,
And swim to night's auspicious noon,
The star-sea ride and swiftly glide
From eventide to eventide,
Whirl through a month that I may say,
"It *is* the Day! It *is* the Day!
My bride comes smiling down this way!"

THE INEVITABLE.

I WILL not sing the pluméd hearse,
Nor weave the cypress in my verse;
The mournful weeping-willow tree
Shall never weave a wreath for me.

Sing, joyous Muse, the blooming rose,
The fountain sparkling as it flows,
Sing life, sing love forever young;
Leave grim, malicious Death unsung.

The Muse drooped low her radiant head,
"The rose is withering," she said;
"The fountain at its source is dry,
And youth, and love and beauty die."

THE INEVITABLE.

And therefore do I bid thee sing
Of pleasure fleet on crimson wing;
Sing of delight, and fill the lay
With laughter, kisses, morn and May.

The Muse began, with blissful art,
To sing the wishes of my heart:
But mocking Death's malicious tongue
A hollow, hideous basso sung.

HINCHMAN'S MILL.

LONELY by Miami's stream,
    Gray in twilight's fading beam,
  Spectral, desolate and still,
Smitten by the storms of years,
Ah! how changed to me appears
    Yonder long-deserted mill.

While the ruin I behold,
Mossy roof and gable old,
    Shadowy 'mid obscuring trees,
Memory's vision, quick and true,
Time's long vista gazing through,
    Unseen pictures dimly sees.

Sees upon the garner floor
Wheat and maize in golden store,—

HINCHMAN'S MILL.

Powdery whiteness everywhere,
Sees a miller short and stout,
Whistling cheerfully about,
    Making merry with his care.

Pleased, he listens to the whirr
Of the swift-revolving burr,
    Deeming brief each busy hour;
Like a stream of finest snow,
Sifting to the bin below,
    Fall the tiny flakes of flour.

Once my childish feet were led
Down some furtive way of dread,
    Through yon broken floor to peer,
Where the fearful waters drift
In a current dark and swift,
    Flying from the angry weir.

Once, with timid step and soft,
Stealthily I climbed aloft,
    Up and up the highest stair;
Iron cogs were rumbling round,
Every vague and awful sound
    Mocked and mumbled at me there.

HINCHMAN'S MILL.

Wonder if those wheels remain,
And would frighten me again?
 Wonder if the miller's dead?
Wonder if his ghost at night
Haunts the stairs, a phantom white?
 Walks the loft, with hollow tread?

Glides the river by the mill,
But the wheels are stark and still,
 Worn and wasting day by day;
So the stream of years will run
When my busy life is done,
 So my task-house shall decay.

THE TUNES DAN HARRISON USED TO PLAY.

OFTTIMES when recollections throng
　　Serenely back from childhood's years,
Awaking thoughts that slumbered long,
　　Compelling smiles or starting tears,
The music of a violin
Seems through my window floating in;
I think I hear from far away,
The tunes Dan Harrison used to play.

Dan Harrison—I see him plain,
　　Beside the roaring, winter hearth,
Playing away with might and main,
　　His honest face aglow with mirth;
And when he laid his bow aside,
"Well done! well done!" he gayly cried;

THE TUNES DAN HARRISON USED TO PLAY.

Well done! well done! indeed were they,
The tunes Dan Harrison used to play.

I do not know what tunes he played,
   I can not name one melody;
His instrument was never made
   In old Cremona o'er the sea;
And yet I sadly, sadly fear
Such tunes I never more may hear,
Some were so mournful, some so gay,
The tunes Dan Harrison used to play.

I have been witness to the skill
   Of many a master of the bow,
But none has had the power to thrill
   Like him I celebrate; and so
I sit and strive, not all in vain,
To hear his minstrelsy again;
And from the past I call to-day
The tunes Dan Harrison used to play.

And with the music, as it floats,
   Seraphic harping faintly blends;
I catch amid the mingling notes
   Familiar voices of old friends;

THE TUNES DAN HARRISON USED TO PLAY.

And all my pensive soul within
Is melted by the violin,
That yields, at fancy's magic sway,
The tunes Dan Harrison used to play.

CHILD LOST.

NINE by the Cathedral clock:
    Chill the air with noxious damps;
Lonesomely from block to block
  In the gloom the bell-man tramps.

    "Oh, yes! oh, yes!
      Child lost! blue eyes,
      Curly hair, pink dress,—
      Child lost! oh, yes!"

Hushed by the pathetic cry,
  Mirth subdues the rising jest,
And a deep, responsive sigh
  Saddens gentle pity's breast.

Many a loving father's heart
  Throbs with home-remembering pain;

CHILD LOST.

Tears to many an eyelid start,
    Summoned by the mournful strain.

As the voice forlorn they hear,
    Tremulous with love's alarms,
Mothers clasp their children dear
    Closer in protecting arms.

Ten the old Cathedral sounds;
    Rain is drizzling in the streets;
Still the bell-man goes his rounds,
    Still the doleful cry repeats:

    "Oh, yes! oh, yes!
      Child lost! blue eyes,
      Curly hair, pink dress,—
    Child lost! oh, yes!"

"Can't my little one be found?
    Are there any tidings, friend?
Is she stolen? Is she drowned?
    Heaven protect her and defend!

"Search the common, search the park,
    Search the door-ways and the halls,

CHILD LOST.

Search the alleys foul and dark,
   Search the empty market stalls!

"Here is gold and silver. See!
   Take it all and welcome, men,
Only find my child for me,
   Give her to my arms again!"

Hark! the old Cathedral bell
   Peals ELEVEN, and it sounds
To the mother, like a knell;
   Still the bell-man goes his rounds.

"Oh, yes! oh, yes!
   Child lost! blue eyes,
Curly hair, pink dress,—
   Child lost! oh, yes!"

Sleepers, half-awakened, deem
   That the lonesome, midnight call,
Startling silence, is a dream,
   And to deeper slumber fall.

But the wailing mother cries,
   "Oh! my darling's curling hair,

CHILD LOST.

Oh! her sweetly smiling eyes,
   Have you sought them everywhere?

"Anguish—agony of dread—
   Breaks my heart and drives me wild!
What if Minnie should be dead!
   Oh, my God! bring home my child!"

TWELVE by the Cathedral clock.
   Dimly flare the midnight lamps,
Drearily from block to block,
   In the rain the bell-man tramps.

"Oh, yes! oh, yes!
   Child lost! blue eyes,
   Curly hair, pink dress,—
Child lost! oh, yes!"

Wanes the night and dawns the day;
   Frenzied mother, weep no more;
Listen! Minnie's laughter gay!
   See her bounding through the door!

"Mother, kiss me—I am here,—
   Safe I slept in Lackey's mill;

CHILD LOST

Was not that a bed-room queer?"
    Sits the mother white and still.

"Mother, you are scared, I know,
    For your fingers shake in mine!
Do not moan and whisper so!
    Ah! your eyes so strangely shine!"

Palsied with a dumb affright,
    Minnie totters, faints, and falls;
Staring toward the morning light,
    Wild the maniac mother calls:

    'Oh, yes! oh, yes!
    Child lost! blue eyes,
    Curly hair, pink dress,—
    Child lost! oh, yes!"

SONGS OF FREEDOM
AND FAITH.

WE THE PEOPLE.

"Its own are all things between earth and sky."
—*Campanella*.

WE the People, not the Crown,
    Not the Surplice nor the Brand,
Noble's crest nor Schoolman's gown,
Burse nor Rostrum, Grange nor Town,—
    We the People rule our Land.

We the People, not the Few,
    High nor low nor middle Class,
High and low and middle too,
Freemen, he and I and you,
    We the Multitude, the Mass.

Dumb we plodded servile years,
    Goaded by the lash of Power;
Groaning, wept a sea of tears;

WE THE PEOPLE.

Lo! at last our day appears!
   Heaven's clock hath struck the hour!

Asia deemed our woe decreed;
   Brahm nor Buddha heard our cry;
Europe heard with scornful heed;
Prince and Pontiff mocked our need,
   Making Christ a bitter lie.

Demagogue nor Demigod
   Shall again control the World;
MAN awoke! disdained the rod,
Spurned the despot whip and prod,
   To the dust his rider hurled.

Man has come unto his own;
   Broken are his bands and bars.
Faith's futurity foreknown,
Domes a sky of promise sown
   Thick with happy-omened stars.

Azure blood and feudal crest,
   Blazon of heraldic scroll,
Coin in coffer, star on breast,—

WE THE PEOPLE.

These are good, but better, best
   Is the rank, the wealth of soul.

Earth grows better growing old,
   Still by happier races trod;
Plato's iron men are gold;
Large humanities unfold;
   Evolution's law is—God.

We the People, cycling slow,
   Up the mount of Progress climb;
Patience points the way we go;
Cloud, or fiery pillar's glow,
   Leads our endless march sublime.

Zealous, not iconoclast,
   We would spare the ancient true;
Life in death is rooted fast;
And the fruitage of the Past
   Is the Passing,—is the New.

We are neither fool nor blind,
   Nihil horde nor rabble mob;
We the People know our mind;

WE THE PEOPLE.

From the heart of human kind,
   All our million pulses throb.

All are wiser than the wise;
   All are better than the good;
All for all can best devise;
We the People sympathize
   With each brother's brotherhood.

We the People know our need,
   Common want of common man;
By our prescience 't is decreed
Who shall follow, who shall lead,
   Who shall execute, who plan.

Congressman and President,
   These are but the People's hands;
Theirs to do and represent
What the head, the Government,—
   What the People's will commands.

What the People will is best.
   When have we our trust belied?
We have builded in the West;

WE THE PEOPLE.

Freedom leans upon our breast;
   Freedom is the People's bride.

We the People—We the State—
   Subject, Sovereign, both in one,—
Trust in Highest Potentate.
Trust, O World, in Us and wait.
   God has willed our will be done.

THE VOICE OF ALL.

YOU will see me at the poll:
　　Never doubt I shall be there;
By the starry flag I swear!
There, and vote with all my soul.
'T is my right, my glory too,
'T is a debt to manhood due,
'T is a duty grave and great,
Owed to Heaven, Home and State.

I shall ne'er forget nor fail;
I shall go through storm or sun;
For my ticket tallies ONE!
ONE will turn the balanced scale;
ONE may choose my candidate;
ONE may change the Nation's fate;

THE VOICE OF ALL.

ONE! but one whose magic might
Throttles Wrong and rescues Right.

I shall vote with brain and heart,
With a thrill of sacred awe
Reason, Liberty, and Law
Charge me do my patriot part;
Bid my conscience make its choice;
Bid me give conviction voice;
As a citizen, a man,
Self-ruled, free, American.

Precious, blood-bought ballot-box!
Keep it pure from every stain;
Guard it e'en till thou be slain,
For 't is holy. DEI VOX.
Voice of God through it is heard,
When it speaks the People's word.
Let it tell the will of all;
Guard it, though the heavens fall.

THE VENAL VOTE.

AND *thou* didst sell thy vote and *thou* didst buy.
    Contempt disdains to point at such as ye.
Slink from the sight of freemen—slink and die.
    Name not the name of Holy Liberty.

Stain not your flag by glancing at its stars.
    Ye are polluted by a shameful crime:
Ye have no right but right to prison bars:
    Go! branded on the forehead for all time.

THE HOME FLAG.

JULY the Fourth. On that proud day I saw,
  To music marching down the gala street,
A scanty regiment of veterans,
Survivors from a hundred battle-fields,
Who knew the home-sick life of weary camp,
The pinch of hunger, and the pain of wounds,
And how the bomb-shell screams. They bore on high,
Brave flags, gunpowder-tanned and bullet-rent,
Pathetic remnants, which to look upon
Brought sudden flood of tears into my eyes,
And made my throat grow big, while loud my heart
Beat like a drum, tuning my footsteps home,
Home to my house,—is't not my castle, too?
Bright in its place upon my book-room wall
My home flag shone, aglow with many stars.
Beneath it sat and read of Paul Revere,

THE HOME FLAG.

My brown-eyed, passionate, and tender boy.
The flag's bright folds baptized his careless curls.
A great emotion trembled in my soul.
I heard a distant cannon's drowsy boom,
And near, I heard a wood-thrush softly sing,
And God seemed intimate with all the world.

A TRIUNE CREED.

I. FAITH.

THE spreading circle of the known,
    That Science strives to bound with laws,
Is but a glowing sparkle thrown
    From God, the radiant central cause.

His mystery is vaster far
    Than knowledge is or e'er can be;
The wheel of Evolution's Car
    Rolls onward through Infinity.

A stilly voice forever sounds
    The lapses of our doubt between:
"Seek not to give Religion bounds,
    Nor limit Faith by forces seen."

A TRIUNE CREED.

II. HOPE.

BEFORE Jehovah was or Jove,
   The Spirit lived that God we name;
Call him the Everlasting Love,
   The potent, all-controlling Same.

His hand forever shall unroll
   Religion's volume unto man;
To every age the sacred scroll
   Reveals Salvation's clearer plan.

From good to better and to best,
   From Myth of Dawn to Fact of Day,
The world progresses, hath progressed,
   And surely shall progress for aye.

III. LOVE.

I HAVE not stricken from my creed
   Nor Buddha, Kung, nor Socrates;
The morning stars that safely lead
   My feet to Bethlehem, are these.

A TRIUNE CREED.

I love Judea's Prince the more
   For loving every Saint and Seer;
The crosses that the Heathen bore
   But make the Christian cross more dear.

I love the Man of Sorrows most
   Because he weeps for all the race;
And promises the Holy Ghost
   To comfort man in every place.

THERE IS NO CASTE IN BLOOD.

> "There is no caste in blood."
> —*The Light of Asia.*

IN Gunga's vale is heard
  Siddartha's sacred word.
Thrill, heart of Hindostan!
Good tidings! Man is man.
The Sudra's eyes grow dim
With tears, for unto him
Thus speaks Siddartha good,
"There is no caste in blood."

Take comfort, humble soul!
The ages hopeward roll;
Time grows compassionate;
Thou art not doomed by Fate;
Religion shall prevail;
Hail! blessed Buddha! hail!

THERE IS NO CASTE IN BLOOD.

Proclaim thy message good,
"There is no caste in blood."

Ye plains of Ind, rejoice
At Love's sweet-sounding voice!
Ye heights of Himalay,
Gleam bright for joy to-day!
The truth to Buddha sent
New lights the Orient,
Presaging all men good:
"There is no caste in blood."

Hereafter, in the West,
Shall walk a Prince more blest,—
The man condemned to bleed
For meek-eyed mercy's creed.
He, Prince of Peace, our Lord,
The Christ, the Incarnate Word,
Shall preach "One Brotherhood!"
"There is no caste in blood."

THE SEEKING SOUL.

WITH yearning soul devout,
   I seek for Good and True;
In labyrinths of doubt,
My bleeding hands stretch out
   For the celestial clue.

Beam on me with Thy face,
   Oh! Light of Lights! and show
My path through this dark place;
Grant me Thy guiding grace,
   That I to Thee may go.

Not for a saint's abode,
   Not for a crown, I pray,
Not for a thornless road,
Not for a lighter load,
   But for the Truth—the Way.

BY THEIR FRUITS.

ABOVE the clash of counter creeds
   These gospel accents swell;
Whoever doeth righteous deeds
   Hath read his Bible well.

Like blossoms of the fragrant spring
   Are adoration's vows;
The tree that pleases God will bring
   Fair fruitage on its boughs.

The holy church is that wherein
   The golden rule controls;
The soul is surely saved from sin
   That lives for other souls.

REVELATION.

'TIS midmost winter, and the umber earth
  Is lost in snow. All yesternight the breath
Of the Ohio lingeringly warm
With impress of Kanawha's southern kiss,
Rose like a soundless sigh or like a soul,
And found a spectral body in the air.
The hoar-frost has transfigured all the vales,
And all the hills, and every house and tree;
Yon rude familiar cottage—nay 't is gone,
Instead, a pearly dream-tent where may dwell
My erewhile neighbors, now immortal sprites.
A spiritual light miraculous,
A universal radiance bathes the scene;
The orchard and the forest rival June
In wealth of magic foliage and flower.
How different from June,—the marble this,

REVELATION.

The pulseless, perfect statue of dead life;
No color, warmth, or passion, no unrest,
All light celestial, beautiful, serene.

I sought no sign to cure my skeptic doubt,
Yet heaven vouchsafed this revelation clear;
The Unknown condescended to these hills
And crowned them with His glory. I have seen,
And I do know Eternal Loveliness.
There is no change. Eternity is now,
The finite is the infinite, and Earth
Is Paradise dim seen through mortal vail.

AN OCTAVE OF SONNETS.

"In sundry moods, 'twas pastime to be bound
Within the Sonnet's scanty plot of ground."
—*Wordsworth.*

AN INDIA SHAWL.

THIS dainty shawl an Eastern shuttle wove,
    Where Ravee's stream winds sunward from
      Cashmere;
By nimble gold 't was borne around the sphere
For him[*] who gave it me in friendly love.
To rival Nature's hues the weaver strove,
For beauty's sake and not barbaric show;
Behold, commingled here, elusive glow
The brilliant, innocent dyes of field and grove.
This silk-soft web was never merchandise;
A charm of peerless art proclaims it rare,
A delicate robe that Majesty would prize,
And India's British Empress well might wear;
'Tis mine for thee within whose beaming eyes
I see love's India, O my queenly Fair.

[*] Joseph Longworth.

PLATO.

PLATO the Greek,—the effulgent Attic mind,
    His name shines brighter as it waxes old;
He changed Philosophy from dross to gold
By poet's alchemy; and he combined
Egypt and Ind and the Hellenic States,
With all the knowledge Cadmus' letters hold,
In Logic's crucible to be refined.
He opened Speculation's splendid gates
To Western ways where Science after trod.
A reign of sweeter Ethics he foretold.
With mild Religion's starry sandals shod,
He walked unfrightened by the awful Fates,
For he believed in the Eternal God,
And life immortal for the human kind.

DANTE.

AFTER READING PARADISO.

HIS sacred muse, on rapture's soaring wings,
   Aspired the radiant empyrean high,
And bore to earth the splendor of the sky.
Durante's spirit to my senses brings
The excessive beauty of transcendent things
That thrill imagination's ear and eye;
With joy I hear the blissful carollings
Of angel hosts in robes of dazzling white.
My soul partakes the poet's ecstasy;
Through all my meditation and my prayer
Steals reminiscence of the Stream of Light,
And of the Rose unutterably fair,
And oh! the three-orbed glory of The One,—
The Love that moves in Heaven the stars and sun.

CARLYLE.

"CARLYLE is dead." Carlyle can never die.
The sovereign genius he to Scotia born;
The scourge of every lofty-crested lie,
How terrible the lightning of his scorn!
His startling voice surprised a wakened age,
Like sudden blast of Gideon's battle-horn!
Heroic music storms along his page!
The strength of Thor is in his verseless song,
The tenderness of woman's loving sigh.
His range from Hades to the Seventh Sky.
Gigantic faculties his bosom throng.
Behold an Idol Breaker much divine.
Bow worshipful before his rugged shrine.
He thought sincerely, and he smote the Wrong.

WAGNER DEAD.

THE music of the Future hath become
　　The music of the Present. Wagner's war
Is over, and his daring hand is numb.
He hath ascended in the Magic Car.
Walhalla takes her latest hero home,
And mortals haste to crown his bust with bays.
Melodious Nature doth the loss bewail
Of him who knew her language, and whose art
Revealed the passionate music of her heart.
Grieved Ocean, roaring on some rocky bar,
Begins a requiem, and the impulsive gale
Its rocky harp of sky-rent mountains plays:
To harmonize the universal dole,
The weeping clouds their solemn thunders roll.

WAGNER'S KAISER MARCH.

WHAT notes are these that from the hush profound
    Thy magic wand, O Master,* summons forth?
Titanic Wagner's art informs the sound:
Hail! multitudinous music of the North!
Exulting laud imperial Kaiser crowned.
Ho! instruments triumphant! trump and drum,
And cymbal clanging where the troopers come!
The Gothic valor now is set to score;
I hear the tramp of Saxon thought unbound,
The victor's cry, disdaining death or wound,—
I hear the saber ring, the cannon roar!
This is the throbbing tune for Halfred's rhyme,
The symphony of glorious war sublime,
The soldier's stormy joy forevermore!

          *Theodore Thomas.

LONGFELLOW AT NAHANT.

I DINED with him one day, the Heart-enchanter,
   On Yankee chowder, fruit, and Shropshire cheese,
And red Burgundy from a quaint decanter;
(Parnassus feasts on substances like these.)
His brow serene was crowned with reverend snows;
On his lapel faint blushed a wayside rose,
The sweet companion of his morning saunter;
The limner Bard* he praised, and honored those
The mated souls who with the muses dwell
On their lone hill near which the Ohio flows;†
Then flew to Spain his fancy migratory;
With glowing lip he told the wondrous spell
Of wise Cervantes' world-delighting story—
The immortal Don, La Mancha's pride and glory.

* T. Buchanan Read. † The Piatts.

UNSUNG.

WHEN comes the Poet whose revealing hand
    Creates the epic of the New World Folk?
Of Saxon People in Mound-Builders' land,
German and British hearts of Western oak.
When cometh he to sing the rugged song
Of Forest-felling and of Scalp-knife war?
Of gold-veins bled, and savage prairie broke?
Of bison scared by steam-winged Palace car?
Of Freedom expiating Slavery's crime?
To sing the song of cis-Atlantic men?
And all the thought and passion of their time?
His verse shall flow magnificently strong;
Like lance's thrust or daring saber stroke
The brilliant wielding of his potent pen.

OCCASIONAL PIECES.

A GENTLE MAN.

I KNEW a gentle man;*
    Alas! his soul has flown;
Now that his tender heart is still,
Pale anguish haunts my own.
His eye, in pity's tears,
Would often saintly swim;
He did to others as he would
That they should do to him.

He suffered many things;
Renounced, forgave, forbore;
And sorrow's crown of thorny stings,
Like Christ, he meekly wore.
At rural toils he strove,
In beauty, joy he sought,

* My Father. Obiit 1871.

A GENTLE MAN.

His solace was in children's words,
And wise men's pondered thought.

He was both meek and brave,
Not haughty and yet proud;
He daily died his soul to save,
And ne'er to Mammon bowed.
E'en as a little child
He entered Heaven's Gate;
I caught his parting smile, which said,
"Be reconciled, and wait."

VICTOR.

WHEN June exhaled her rose-sweet breath,
    And earth in sunshine smiled,
Untimely came intrusive Death,
    And robbed us of our child.

The pallid specter, frozen Sleep,
    To Victor's cradle stole,
And kissed the babe to silence deep,
    Then lured away his soul.

As some pathetic star declines,
    Slow-fading down the sky;
As wastes a dew-drop while it shines,
    So did our darling die.

Ah, sweeter than the violet frail,
    Frost-slain on April's breast,

VICTOR.

And purer than the snow-drop pale,
    The unbreathing cherub's rest.

Oh, hapless Victor! name of pride!
    Dear hands,—poor, little feet;
No thorn you found, no path you tried;
    Fond heart! no more 't will beat.

Our eyes grew numb with tearless woe,
    Prayer swooned upon our tongue,
As to your lips of smiling snow
    Our hopeless kisses clung.

Oh, mournful change and utter loss!
    Sweet innocent, return
Or, angels, guide my faith across
    The grave his state to learn.

I fear he mutely pines to come
    Where we who love him are;
His mother's bosom is his home,
    Not some strange heaven far.

All silent is the stolid sky,
    The saints no message send;

VICTOR.

My lamentation and my cry
  To heedless void ascend.

My heart, my weeping, bleeding heart,
  Wails at the door of fate;
And faints in darkness and apart,
  Bereft and desolate.

I only find, where'er I grope,
  A cradle and a pall;
Find, at the gloomy verge of hope,
  A grave—and that is all.

An empty cradle and a lone,
  Small mound of chilly sod,
O'er which I bow and vainly moan
  To move the heart of God.

THE CONCORD SEER.

THE Transcendentalist—he now transcends
The cloud of death to join immortal friends.
The Saadi of the West, the Saint, the Sage,
The north-sprung Plato of an un-Greek age,
Hath changed his habitation. Lo! the shore
Of time and matter bears his form no more.
On earth he has become that sacred thing
A living Book for mankind's bettering;
A Book immortal, yet his other ghost
Takes note authentic of the unknown coast.
Ah! joy serene! there doth he recognize
Congenial souls foreknown "polite and wise."
Two bards were first to hail his risen wraith,
One sang the Psalm of Life, one that of Death;
Then mystic Hawthorne took his willing hand,
As Virgil Dante's in the Shadow Land.

THE CONCORD SEER.

Now haply doth his converse reconcile
Momentous discords with redeemed Carlyle.
Perhaps in Soul's consortable domain
He meets the shade of erudite Montaigne;
Or German-Grecian Goethe shows the way
To Fields Elysian where the Ancients stray.
By some Illissus clear, of Paradise,
Where grass is green and stately plane trees rise,
May sit, discoursing calm philosophies,
The Concord Seer with Athen's Socrates.

THE POET OF CLOVERNOOK.

Read at the celebration of ALICE CARY's Birthday, to the children of the Public Schools of Cincinnati, April 26, 1880.

A POET born, not made,
   By Nature taught, she knew,
And knowing, still obeyed
   The Beautiful, the True.

Hers was the seeing eye,
   The sympathetic heart,
The subtle art whereby
   Lone genius summons art.

She caught the primal charm
   Of every season's scene,—
Of river, cottage, farm,
   Blue sky, and woodland green.

THE POET OF CLOVERNOOK.

Baptized in Sorrow's stream,
  She sang, how sweetly well,
Of true Love's tender dream,
  And sad Death's asphodel.

Her pensive muse has fled
  From hill and meadow-brook,
No more her footsteps tread
  Thy paths, fair Clovernook.

No more may she behold
  The dew-crowned summer morn,
On wings of sunrise gold,
  Fly o'er the bending corn.

No more her mournful gaze,
  On autumn eves, shall mark
Red twilight's smoldering rays
  Slow westering to the dark.

Nor note of joyous bird,
  Nor April's fragrant breath,
Nor tear, nor loving word,
  May break the spell of Death.

THE POET OF CLOVERNOOK.

Sleep on! and take thy rest,
  In Greenwood, by the sea.
Dear Poet of the West,
  Thy West remembers thee.

THE PATRIOT'S MEED.

FEBRUARY 22, 1881.

OH keep their memory green, who led
    A fainting Nation's hope forlorn:
What blows they gave! What blood they shed!
    What pangs their patience learned to scorn!

The patriot saviors! Swift they rose
    The primal rights of man to save!
Their bleeding feet and tattered clothes
    Are freedom's emblems of the brave.

Remember Valor's piteous plight
    In Valley Forge, the camp of prayer;
Mark Wanhope's agonizing night,
    Storm-mocked on frozen Delaware.

THE PATRIOT'S MEED.

My heart reveres a stately name,
   Which, bright and fadeless as a star,
Shines lambent in the sky of fame,
   Above remembered clouds of war.

Still as his birthday circles round,
   The people's hearts foreknow the time;
Sound, loud majestic music, sound!
   And happy bells, rejoicing, chime!

And ye, stern cannon, jar the earth!
   For it is meet your echoing boom
Should celebrate our Freedom's birth,
   And repronounce Oppression's doom.

A GIFT ACKNOWLEDGED.

Written in illness, to the boys who sent me a basket of flowers, February 19, 1881.

YOUR Winter gift of bud and bloom
    Took nature by surprise;
'T was sudden Summer in my room,
    And April in my eyes.

The kindly mist a moment stole
    The flowers from my view,
But lo! they blossomed in my soul,
    Where love their fragrance knew.

Fair embassy! their smiles I greet,
    Camellia, pink and rose;
I understand the message sweet
    Their gentle hearts enclose.

A GIFT ACKNOWLEDGED.

Their winsome beauty gladdens me
  With this immortal truth:
No age can quite unhappy be
  That still remembers youth.

Dear boys! companions! friends sincere!
  More warm and true than men,
I thank you most because my tear
  Made me a boy again.

FOREST SONG.

Read at the first meeting of the AMERICAN FORESTRY CONGRESS, in Music Hall, Cincinnati, April, 19, 1882.

A SONG for the beautiful trees!
    A song for the forest grand,
The Garden of God's own hand,
The pride of His centuries.
Hurrah! for the kingly oak,
    For the maple, the sylvan queen,
For the lords of the emerald cloak,
    For the ladies in living green.

For the beautiful trees a song,
    The peers of a glorious realm,
    The linden, the ash, and the elm,
The poplar stately and strong.

FOREST SONG.

Hurrah! for the beech tree trim,
   For the hickory staunch at core,
For the locust thorny and grim,
   For the silvery sycamore.

A song for the palm,—the pine,
   And for every tree that grows
   From the desolate zone of snows
To the zone of the burning line;
Hurrah! for the warders proud
   Of the mountain-side and vale,
That challenge the thunder cloud,
   And buffet the stormy gale.

A song for the forest aisled,
   With its Gothic roof sublime,
   The solemn temple of Time,
Where man becometh a child,
As he listens the anthem-roll
   Of the wind in the solitude,
The hymn which telleth his soul
   That God is the voice of the wood.

So long as the rivers flow,
   So long as the mountains rise,

FOREST SONG.

May the forest sing to the skies,
And shelter the earth below;
Hurrah! for the beautiful trees!
Hurrah! for the forest grand,
The pride of His centuries,
The Garden of God's own hand.

FOR MY CHILDREN.

THE SCHOOL GIRL.

FROM some sweet home, the morning train
    Brings to the city,
Five days a week, in sun or rain,
Returning like a song's refrain,
    A school girl pretty.

A wild flower's unaffected grace
    Is dainty miss's,
Yet, in her shy, expressive face,
The touch of urban arts I trace,—
    And artifices.

No one, but she and Heaven, knows
    Of what she's thinking;

THE SCHOOL GIRL.

It may be either books or beaux,
Fine scholarship or stylish clothes,
    Per cents or prinking.

How happy must the household be,
    This morn who kissed her;
Not every one can make so free;
Who sees her, inly wishes she
    Were his own sister.

How favored is the book she cons,
    The slate she uses,
The hat she lightly doffs and dons,
The orient sun-shade that she owns,
    The desk she chooses.

Is she familiar with the wars
    Of Julius Cæsar?
Do crucibles and Leyden jars,
And French, and earth, and sun, and stars,
    And Euclid, please her?

She studies music, I opine;
    O day of knowledge!
And all the other arts divine,

THE SCHOOL GIRL.

Of imitation and design,
  Taught in the college.

A charm attends her everywhere;
  A sense of beauty;
Care smiles to see her free of care;
The hard heart loves her unaware;
  Age pays her duty.

She is protected by the sky;
  Good spirits tend her;
Her innocence is panoply;
God's wrath must on the miscreant lie,
  Who dares offend her!

FLORA'S FAVORITE.

HATTIE is the first to seek
  March-rime in the woodland bleak;
First to mourn the aster's death,
Withered by November's breath;
All the corols of the wild
Court the sympathetic child;
Every leafy knoll she knows
Where the coy spring-beauty grows;
Adder-tongues for her unfold
Lily-bells of pearl or gold.
None in April woods so soon
Greets the snowy, frail puccoon.
In the dingle gray she sees
Slender-stem'd anemones,—

From the breast of Summer takes
Buttercups and plumy brakes,
And the fringed Miami Mist,
Hued with paly amethyst.

Lilies on their pliant stalks
Bow the way the maiden walks;
Roses to her pathway lean,
Queens saluting lovelier queen;
Pinks and pansies at her feet
By their fragrance her entreat;
All the garden graces cry
"Pluck me," as she dances by,
Knowing that her fingers cull
But to make more beautiful.
Blossoms live and die for this—
Being beauteous is their bliss.
Hattie's art is nature taught
By diviner maiden thought;
Flora's gifts are so combined
By her fantasy refined,
That they cluster to the view
Musical in form and hue;
Thus do sounds that singly please,
Join in chordant melodies,

FLORA'S FAVORITE.

So do gathered fancies twine,
Blended in the rhythmic line;
Like a perfect lyric lay,
Hattie's exquisite bouquet.

THE SACRED SNOW.

WE took a walk in Winter woods,
   My little lad and I.
The hills and hollows all were pearl,
   And sapphire all the sky.

Before guerrilla winds we saw
   The skurrying drift retreat;
We talked of budded roots that lay
   Asleep beneath our feet.

We spoke of how, last year, in May,
   One sunny bank we found,
Where wind-flowers stood in fairy crowds,
   To charm the gladdened ground.

A subtile feeling checked the boy,—
   His small hand held me back,

THE SACRED SNOW.

With mute appeal that we should tread
    The wood-path's beaten track.

"My child, 't is pleasanter to break
    New pathways as we go."
He said, "I do not like to spoil
    The beauty of the snow."

Ah, vision clear, and instinct fine!
    To recognize, to spare,
Earth's robe resplendent, wove on high
    By fingers of the air!

Thou dost in evanescent things
    A law eternal find;
The spirit of the Lovely calls
    Unto thy answering mind.

No test of critic art, to thee
    Reveals the line of grace;
Before thine eyes the Beautiful
    Unveils her heavenly face.

Like snow on heaven-kissing hills,
    Dear boy, upon thee lies

THE SACRED SNOW.

The purity that love Divine
  Sheds down from Paradise.

As rounding years from blooming Spring
  To frost-crowned Winter roll,
Oh, may no trail of evil mar
  The whiteness of thy soul!

FAIRY LAND.

HARD by our cottage sleeps a brown ravine,
  Close guarded now by Summer boscage green.
Oft do I hear at midday's solemn hush,
From out its heart the note of hermit-thrush.
Nursed by young May, the adder-tongue grows there,
And frail diletra breathes the scented air.
A haunt it seems for elfin revels planned,
And so the children name it Fairy Land.

There spring the red-bud and the mulberry,
The water-beech, the gold-plumed buckeye tree,
The rank wild-cherry, and the thorny haw,
The graceful locust and the proud pawpaw;
One sycamore lifts high its limbs of snow,
And at its feet. bloom-laden elders grow.

FAIRY LAND.

Aloof, three sugar-maples sentry stand
To guard the entrance of the Fairy Land.

O'er all the glen the busy grape-vine weaves
A canopy of interlacing leaves,
Whereon the children, rocked by breezes, lie,
And shout into the blue face of the sky,
Until the startled cat-birds, safely bold,
Forget to sing, and insolently scold;—
In morning's blush, by roseate æther spanned,
A bower of dew-drops, glitters Fairy Land.

When dusk descends, the fairy host delight,
In form of fire-flies, to bestar the night;
While melancholy tree-toads shrill the throat,
And myriad insects sound an irksome note.
Perchance the screech-owl hurtles on its prey,
And nestling birdies shiver with dismay;
For evil things some dreadful hours command,
Though holy stars keep watch o'er Fairy Land.

All spells lurk there, the evil and the good,
Down in the hollow of the spriteful wood.
There sky brings earth distillings of the sea;
The moon plies there her midnight witchery;

FAIRY LAND.

Time slumbers there; there Life and Beauty sport,
And Death holds there his grim, fantastic court.
No ghost may tell, no mortal understand,
The mystic wonders of our Fairy Land?

A BOY'S HEAVEN.

MEMORY the picture brings
    Fancy drew of Heaven's joy,
  For a solitary boy,
Dreaming of transmundane things.

Not a golden city's glare,
    Pearly gates and jasper walls,
    Splendid in the light that falls
Dazzling down the crystal air.

But an Eden realm of nooks,
    Drooping vines and babbling streams,
    Airy harps and twilight beams,
Angel loves and story-books.

THE READERS.

"Come hither, my ten years' maiden;
    On what do you ponder so much?"

"I am reading in Tanglewood Stories,
    The tale of the 'Golden Touch.'"

"Ah! Hattie, my flax-haired darling,
    How buried in study you seem."

"I am reading in 'Tales from Shakespeare,'
    Of Puck in 'Midsummer Night's Dream.'"

"And there on the sofa is Mayo;
    My laddie, what pleases you so?"

"This picture and fable in Æsop,—
    See here,—of the Pitcher and Crow."

THE READERS.

"Come hither, my dream-eyed baby,
    You're falling asleep on the floor!"

"I'm reading in 'Sing Song,' papa,—
    I wish you would read me some more."

WAG.

He was only a dog, and a mongrel at that,
    And worthless and troublesome, lazy and fat,—
  Was Wag, who died yesterday night;
Yet now that his barking forever is o'er,
And his caudal appendage can waggle no more,
  His elegy I will indite.

'T was seldom authority mastered his will;
He always was noisy when bid to be still;
  He slumbered while danger was near;
He ran after chickens against all command;
When ordered to "seek," he would heedlessly stand;
  His principal passion was fear.

From morning till night he would dig in the ground
To get at a rabbit, but when it was found,

WAG.

In terror he took to his heels;
But there was one duty he never did shun,
From that naught could drive him, to that he would run:
    Wag never neglected his meals.

The tax that I paid the police on his poll,
Of a dollar a year, I begrudged in my soul,
    For Wag I thought dear at a cent;
And once, in my hardness, I gloomily said,
"I wish that the no-account puppy was dead!"
    But now he *is* dead, I repent.

Wag came from Kentucky, a waif, bundled up,
And packed in a basket, a charity pup,—
    In pity we warmed him and fed;
The only return that his nature could give,
For preserving his life, was serenely to live,
    Content with his board and his bed.

He was kind to the dogs upon Tusculum Hill,
They all thought of Wag with fraternal good will,
    From coach dog to commonest cur.
He was grateful to *people* who treated him right,
And for his young mistress he even would fight,—
    But not lose his dinner—for her.

WAG.

I miss his black body curled up and asleep;
I miss his contortions, his bark and his leap;
    And the sound of his gnawing at bones;
The very same night that the Pope died at Rome,*
Poor Wag, all alone, in the wash-house at home,
    Yielded up his last, shivering moans.

And when to the children, next morning, I said,
As they sat at the table, "Yes, Wag he is dead,"
    There was not a dry eye in the room;
And Auntie began, with remorse, to recall
How lately she 'd driven deceased from the hall,
    With scoldings and blows of a broom.

Now Wag is asleep near an apple-tree old,
And a dog-rose shall blossom above his dear mold,
    And there shall a tablet be set;
For though but a dog, and a mongrel at that,
And worthless, and idle, and lazy, and fat—
    Poor Wag was *our dog*, and a pet.

* February 7, 1878.

DONATELLO.

WHO will capture Donatello,
 Mary's cat?
Fierce, ungovernable fellow,
Musical as Leporello,—
 Sharp and flat;
Terrible in a duello.

Ragamuffin, have you met a
 Maltese cat?
Ancestored in old Valetta,
Where brown dames in black faldetta,
 Walk and chat.
Hot his blood as flame of Etna.

Beautiful, romantic, splendid
 Southern cat!

DONATELLO.

To the forest, unattended,
Robber Donatello wended;
    Bird and bat,
Rabbit, mole and mink, he rended.

Savage wildwood his unbounded
    Habitat;
By no man or mastiff hounded,
By the midnight mirk surrounded—
    Think of that!
Oft his caterwaul he sounded.

Freedom to the gallant fellow.
    Exeat!
Victor in each fierce duello,
Midnight, mad-cap Leporello!
    Roving cat!
Graceless, graceful Donatello!

ETCHINGS BY THE WAY:

STUDIES IN REALISM.

Sing what thy heart and vision meet,
And gild the muse-neglected street.

THE OPEN SECRET.

THE August sun, malign, from midday sky
  Glares at the world, a lurid, wrathful eye.
The street-car rumbles in a dusty cloud;
On flinty stones the horseshoes clatter loud;
A drowsy spirit haunts the atmosphere,
No one is moved to speak or wills to hear;
I almost sleep, when sudden every sense
Roused by a vision, casts off somnolence.
Behold a damsel who with bounding feet
Makes eager haste the speeding car to meet.
Her free locks flow neglected, and her dress
Shows working-day's disordered gracefulness;
Conspicuous beauty dignifies the maid,
Such arms as hers Nausicaä sure displayed.
What ails our young conductor? For his eyes
This earth-foam Aphrodite brings surprise.

THE OPEN SECRET.

She thrusts into his hands two apples red,
The car rolls on! the dust-born nymph has fled!
Our young conductor's cheek reflects the flush
Of those fair apples, roseate Maiden's Blush;
He thinks no one has seen,—and as for me,
For all the world I would not seem to see;
By Love's contrivance or by happy chance
The passengers remain in sullen trance,
And so see nothing. Only one old dame
Reads in my face confusion and self-blame,
Of which she, subtly guilty, knows the reason;
She, smiling, says: " Nice apples, sir, this season.

A SNOW BIRD.

IT was a Winter morning, cold as death;
A spectral mist pale gleamed my frozen breath;
The savage North's assailing arrows fierce
My very heart's warm center strove to pierce.
Beside the curbstone, in a gusty whirl
Of dust and snow-drift, stood a little girl.
The piteous tears ran down her baby face;
In dumb despair she stood, nor moved a pace.
Her flying curls and fluttering short dress
The signals seemed of most forlorn distress.
Her naked hands, all purple with the cold,
A naked, china doll did fondly hold.
"What is the matter, sissy, that you cry?"
Her chill-cramped lips made dolefullest reply:
"I am so cold, and I do n't know the way."
That was the most her helplessness could say.

A SNOW BIRD.

Erelong, before a laughing, ruddy flame,
She stood by me and shyly told her name.
I led the strayling to her mother's door,
And in she flew. I never saw her more.

On frigid days, when Winter scoffs the sun,
I often think about that tiny one.
She comes into my heart and sobbing stands,
An ice-cold dolly in her purple hands;
I see her shiver, and I hear her say:
"I am so cold, and I don't know the way."

A WHARF RAT.

ONE day in March I saw a lean boy standing
　　On Water Street, down by the Steamboat Landing.
All rags he was and tatters; and his features
They were but skin and bone, like some dried creature's;
One foot was bare, the other wore a stocking:
He was a sight both picturesque and shocking.
Ten years of age he might have been, or younger;
His eyes were bright with fever light of hunger;
His gaze he fastened with a wistful staring
Upon an orange that a man was paring.

The man tossed him an orange big and yellow;
You should have seen that famine-shrunken fellow:
He skipped along the frosty wharf, not heeding
How that glad prank did bruise his foot to bleeding;

A WHARF RAT.

He held the fruit aloft for fond inspection,
Then hugged it close with ravenous affection;
Then, seated on an anchor, at his leisure
Sucked fragrant draughts of epicurean pleasure.

I looked upon the man who caused this gladness;
He glanced aside with smile of thoughtful sadness.

THE UPSET.

ENFORCED pursuit of silver eagles fleet
　　Gave early haste to my reluctant feet,
And so it chanced I hurried—I and Care—
At sunrise down a city thoroughfare;
But, by the grace of some directing fay,
I met a sight that gladdened me all day.

I saw a beer-plump Saxon—Bacchus' son—
His red, round face the symbol of slow fun;
Unconscious he of all 'twixt sky and earth
Except one soul-engrossing cause of mirth.
He dragged a painted sled, and, perched thereon,
Sat snug a three years' maiden bright as dawn.
And happy as the sparrows chirping round,
Crumb hunting near her on the snowy ground.

THE UPSET.

A sudden turn! a laughing cry, and lo!
The sled upsets, and Mädchen prints the snow.
She laughs; I laugh; loud ha-ha's Bacchus' son;
Then gravely he,—"By yolly! dot vas fun."

A MIRACLE.

WITH fingers long and thin, a crooked crone
    From frozen garbage dug a meaty bone.
A stranger passing saw the wretched dame,
And less in charity than human shame
He dropped a silver coin in stealthy wise
As if it might have fallen from the skies,
Upon the hand that shivered for the meat
Rejected from the board for dogs to eat.

As from his deed the blushing stranger ran,
Up rose the woman with a visage wan;
Her grateful eyes sought heaven. God was there;—
He is a God who hears and answers prayer.

PROTOPLASM.

A THING of automatic grace,
It minced along at leisure pace,
With shining shoes upon Its feet,
And on Its locks pomatum sweet.
An ulster wondrous gay It wore,
With dainty trimmings down before,
A super-stylish hat did rest
Above Its ears. Its neck was dressed
With looking-glass-fatiguing care.
Upon Its hands were stretched a pair
Of lemon kids; and It did twirl
A slender cane with head of pearl,
And smoked a tiny cigarette,
And bowed to ladies that It met.

PROTOPLASM.

The curious creature made me think
Of evolution's Missing Link:
So like a man in act and shape,
Yet unmistakably—an ape.

IN THE LIBRARY.

"On bokes for to rede I me delyte."
— *Chaucer.*

WITH BOOKS.

> " .   Loved associates, chiefs of elder art,
> Teachers of wisdom." . . .
>
> *—Roscoe.*

1.

ONCE more the task-imposing sun
   His proud, imperious course has run.
I saw his blood-red, royal crown
Beyond the dreary hills sink down;
While from a chariot of cloud,
Her stormy clarion sounding loud,
The Amazonian Night made war
Against the moon and every star.

My jealous curtains, drooping, hide
Repose within from storm outside.
Rave on, thou wintry tempest, beat
The flying snow from street to street;

WITH BOOKS.

Against the rattling shutter dash,
And madly buffet window-sash;
Thy baffled pinions strive in vain
My still retreat serene to gain.
A safe redoubt, this study chair,
From arrows of the icy air;
My tranquil Argand's yellow ray
Creates a supernatural day;
My Youghiogheny sunshine glows
Defiance to the Boreal snows,
And, flushing, fills my tropic room
With rays that make the roses bloom.

Hence, haggard cares that vex the day,
Blind aches of head and heart, away!
Vague sorrows that the memory haunt,
Pale ghosts of early griefs, avaunt!
Forebodings of disastrous things,
Ye phantom brood, take wings, take wings!
All sordid thoughts of loss or gain,
Alluring hopes, ambitions vain,
Delusive dreams—whate'er ye be,
Depart, and leave my spirit free,
For I would consecrate the hour
To Books and their restoring power!

WITH BOOKS.

II.

Here, in my social solitude,
I make a new Beatitude;
And, Blessèd are the Books, I say,
The Muses' harvest sheaves are they;
They are the vials that contain
The attar of Time's heart and brain;
The sacred lanterns that emit
The light of science, wisdom, wit;
The caskets and the shrines that hold
Thought's diadems, and learning's gold;
The full-brimmed beakers whence are quaffed
Imagination's sparkling draught;
The living fountain-heads where move
Deep waters of perennial love.

Enchanted heroes of the pen,
These Books are living souls of men:
Awake! illustrious guests, spell-bound,
Ye sons of genius, laurel crowned,
Your long, mysterious silence break;
I conjure you, arouse! awake!
Lo! from each scroll and massy tome

WITH BOOKS.

The spirits of the masters come!
They consecrate my humble home!
Immortal sages, seers **and bards,**
They utter inspiration's words;
They whisper meanings manifold
That printed pages never told;
They break the esoteric seal,
And occult mysteries reveal;
My marred ideals they renew;
They speak, they sing the good and true;
As many stars give one pure **light,**
Their diverse messages unite;
Their lofty faith and converse high
Assure me, soul can never die.

III.

My Youghiogheny coal aglow
Illumes my treasures row on row.
There Plato stands, half-deified;
There Burke and Bacon, side by side;
Intense Carlyle by Goethe great;
There Shakespeare grand—for him no mate;
Montaigne and white-light Emerson;

Cervantes, Spain's Immortal One;
Wit Fielding and French Hugo, too,
Elected with the Golden Few.
There genial Dickens, clad in green,
Beside romantic Scott is seen.
Satiric Thackeray is there,
And introspective Hawthorne rare.
The poets, too, a troop divine,
From honored shelves and alcoves shine.
And all these precious leaves are mine.

IV.

No book-worm blind and cold am I,
No friend to grim misanthropy.
That author best contents my mind
Who draws me nearest to mankind.
Not with a scientific greed,
For store of useful facts I read,
Not with a pedant's pride, to know,
That I my ample lore may show;
Not with a worldling's lust of gain,
To gather gold by moil of brain;
Not with the critic's art, to scan,

And praise or blame because I can;—
Not do I pore for ends like these,
I read my books myself to please.
The wise King Solomon, I wis,
Said ne'er a sager thing than this:
"Eat honey, thou, for it is good."
Sweet reading is a dainty food,
Good honey is my book to me—
My author is good honey bee;
Good honey, and because 'tis sweet,
That is the reason why I eat.

v.

Reposing in my charmèd chair
I exorcise the demon Care;
All yesterdays are ever gone,
And never did to-morrow dawn.
Is not the present infinite?
And here, immortal, let me sit.
Without is black December night,
Within is summer warmth and light;
I bend my fond, contented looks
On glinting titles of my books,

WITH BOOKS.

As from the shelves they shine to me
In mute and dreamy sympathy
And in my social solitude
I make a new Beatitude,
And, Blessed are the Books, I say,
For honey of the soul are they.

THE GENIUS OF THE PRESS.

I SAW the Genius of the Press,
   A stalwart form, majestic, grand;
All kings concede him kingliness,
And he can curse and he can bless;
   His armies camp in every land.

His Argus eyes close not in sleep,
   His hands Briærian never rest,
Above the height, below the deep,
His lightning-footed angels leap,
   To North and South and East and West.

He hangs the electric lamps of Fact
   Aloft to light the world of men;
Revealing thought and word and act,
The labyrinth of Things is tracked;
   And Truth triumphant wields her pen.

DEFOE IN THE PILLORY.

When Defoe, for writing a brave book, was led to the pillory, a vast crowd attended him. They garlanded the pillory with flowers, and continued to cheer the prisoner, and to drink his health. The leader of the mob is supposed to speak in the following verses.

ON to the Pillory, ho!
    To punish bold Daniel Defoe!
Come on to the place
Of shame and disgrace!
Bring rose-garlands sweet,
To cast at his feet!
Pour rosy wine, ho!
Here's to Daniel Defoe!

On to the Pillory, ho!
To punish bold Daniel Defoe!

DEFOE IN THE PILLORY.

His fate he has earned,
His book we have burned,
That its soul may fly free!
One and all, come and see
Great London's brave show!
Here's to Daniel Defoe!

On to the Pillory, ho!
To punish bold Daniel Defoe!
Shout him greeting full loud!
Sing his praise to the crowd!
The sentries may swear,
But what do we care?
More roses we'll throw!
Here's to Daniel Defoe!

On to the Pillory, ho!
To punish rogue Daniel Defoe!
Pelt him, maidens and men!
For he thinks with a pen,
And his thought is too free!
God bless him! See! See!!
Fill glasses! Fill, ho!
Here's to Daniel Defoe!

www.ingramcontent.com/pod-product-compliance
Lightning Source LLC
Chambersburg PA
CBHW020108170426
43199CB00009B/448